IN THE SIMPLE MORNING LIGHT

A Meditation Manual

Barbara Rohde

Boston
Skinner House Books

Printed in the USA.

Design by Suzanne Morgan
Edited by Brenda Wong

10 9 8 7 6 5 4 3 2 1
99 98 97 96 95 94

Rohde, Barbara, 1925-
    In the simple morning light : a meditation manual /
Barbara Rohde.
        p. cm.
    Includes bibliographical references
    ISBN 1-55896-275-1
    1. Unitarian Universalist churches—Prayer books
    and devotions—English. 2. Spiritual life—Unitarian
    Universalist churches—Meditations. I. Title.
BX9855.R64 1994
242—dc20   93-40866
                                                    CIP

For Kermit, with love and gratitude.

"We think of such men
and the stone in our breast is dissolved
we take heart once more."
                              —Daniel Berrigan

CONTENTS

I am a writer not a minister, but I think our callings have much in common. We try to witness to what we see. We are always saying, "Here, let me lend you my eyes."

When Emerson suggests that true preachers deal out to people their lives—"life passed through the fire of thought"—I think he is speaking of writers as well.

Both preachers and writers have a stubborn faith that in reflecting on our lives, chaotic as they are, we may find meaning. We have the audacious belief that if we can only get the right words in the right order, we can share that meaning, bridge the vast chasms that separate one human being from another. We might even help to heal what Thomas Merton calls "this body of broken bones."

In our better moments we have the wisdom to laugh at our own audacity, but not to abandon it.

The title for this collection comes from a favorite poem of mine by Stephen Spender. It reflects both my gratitude for the clarity of "the simple morning light" and the fact that most of these pieces began there.

One hears so much about the calamities of growing old that at sixty I began to make a list of the things that I like about my advancing years. My younger friends suggested that I was merely playing Pollyana. My older friends gently pointed out that my list might grow shorter as my life grows longer. Still, I made my list.

At the head of my list was this remarkable discovery: I was beginning to find the foibles of my friends and relatives endearing.

I could understand how, after observing the real tragedies of life for two-thirds of a century, one would become more tolerant of minor irritations. In a world filled with the suffering of the hungry and the homeless and the victims of violence, the cap left off the tooth-paste tube does not loom very large.

But my fondness for these foibles came as a surprise to me. I suppose I finally have come to understand that when one loves, one loves the whole person, a person defined by foibles as well as strengths. Of course, there is still the flash of irritation, but these days when we say, "Isn't that just like him," more often than not, we say it with affection, with the same pleasure of recognition as when the letter in the mailbox is addressed in familiar handwriting.

Perhaps every long marriage follows these five stages: 1. Darling, you are perfect. 2. Good grief! You seem to have a few foibles. 3. Let me help you get rid of your foibles so you will indeed be perfect. 4. Okay, I love you in spite of your foibles. 5. I can't believe this has happened. I sometimes love you because of your foibles.

I recently made the wonderful discovery that "foible" originally meant the weak part of a sword, from the center to the tip, while "forte" referred to the sword's stronger part. That says something to me about accepting our weaknesses while holding on to our strengths. Who would want to go out to meet a dragon with only half a sword?

When our oldest child was five years old, she walked into the kitchen one morning and announced, "I haven't made my decision yet about heaven."

I was somewhat startled. Heaven wasn't a very big topic of conversation in our house, and one wouldn't expect a small person carrying Raggedy Ann by one arm to be thinking much about it.

But I said, "What do you mean, you haven't made your decision?" She said, "I don't know whether you go there when you die or whether you just lie down dead forever." She paused for a minute and added, "And that's why I think it is sometimes hard to be a person."

What is remarkable about that conversation is not so much that a five year old was wrestling with questions of immortality, nor that she already had a sense that life was not always peaches and cream, but that she had some understanding, even at five, that one's personhood is always at issue. Will I become a person? Will I become the person I am intended to become? Will I become a person who can respond to what I am called to do? When I lose my sense of self, will something, someone, call me back?

The task of becoming a person is what life is all about. The care that helps others become their true selves is what parenthood is about, what the ministry is about. I suppose what led most of us to Unitarian Universalism is our understanding that the central question of religion is not whether one lives forever but whether one lives.

While lying close to death in intensive care, with a dozen tubes stuck into my body—to drain me, to nourish me, to help me breathe, to monitor my heart— I was surprised by how much anger I felt. Later, when the things done to me made rational sense, as part of the regime to keep me alive, I was embarrassed by my anger. But at the time I merely raged inside.

One morning, I woke up and, for the first time after the surgery, looked around the room. One wall looked out on the nursing station in the hall. Ahead of me was a blank wall with only a darkened television set. I did not know what was behind me. I hadn't the strength to turn around.

In the fourth wall was the only window, which I assumed must look out on the green hills of Oregon. I did not know for sure because of a "thing" that blocked my view. "Isn't it just like this dumb hospital," I thought to myself. "The only window I can look out and they park this thing in the way."

Later I realized that the "thing" was the respirator that kept me breathing—and alive. I was angrier still with the rocking bed, which was to help me avoid pneumonia. How I hated that bed. Each time it rocked I was sure it would throw me out onto the cold floor. I found myself looking forward to the painful changing of dressings, merely because the bed would stop rocking.

After I became well, it occurred to me that the anger had been a good thing—one of the last struggles of my spirit to stay alive. I resolved to remember that lesson. In my dealings with angry people, it might help me to keep in mind that there is wisdom in anger even when there is not rationality. In my better moments I might try to see beyond red-faced anger to see what this suffering spirit might need so achingly.

If I could, I would go to them
And say, "It was only a dream."
I would sit beside them, and hold
Them in their dark, and let their tears
Fall on the soft sleeves of my gown.
I would kiss their hair. I would talk
Softly to them. I would tell them
The secrets of fireflies and stars
And the frost-lace on the windows
And the harvesting of corn.

I would sing the grandfather's songs.
I would bring small gifts in my hand:
White spiraled shells and crimson leaves,
Smooth stones, a hyacinth, a peach.
Then we would stand by the window,
Our arms around each other's waists.
We would breathe in the cold night air.
We would make promises and wait
Silently. Still. Listening for
The bright, brave, astonishing light.

Of course truth is hard.
It is a rock.
Yet I do not think it will fall upon me
And crush me.
I do not think they can hammer it to bits
And stone me.

Help me place the rock in the strong current
Of these rushing waters.
I must climb upon it.
I must know how truth feels.
When I plunge naked

Into the bright depth of these waters,
I must know how truth feels.
When I am swept by the cold fury of these waters,
I must know, with my whole being, how truth feels.
I shall remember how truth feels.

I praise the rock.
I praise the river.
I fear the drought
More than death by water.

My husband and I had been at a small hotel in Bergen for two days before we discovered the stairway.

We had known it was there, of course. We had seen the sign, if not the thing itself. But we used the elevator. Saved time, we thought, and the energy we needed for exploring that charming Norwegian town on misty October days.

After breakfast on the third day, when the elevator seemed slow in arriving, my husband decided to walk up. He was waiting at the elevator door when I—and the elevator—arrived on the fourth floor. "Let me show you something," he said, and led me back down the stairs he had just come up.

I was dazzled. Instead of the sterile, institutional look of most hotel stairways, this one had the warm beauty of an art-lover's home. There were bright paintings on all the walls, and at each landing a rug in jeweled tones, a table with fresh flowers, an exquisite chair or two. When we reached the first floor, we walked up again, filled with energy, drinking in the beauty.

"We might have missed this," I said.

"Have to be careful about saving time and losing life," he said.

One summer morning—the morning of our forty-fifth wedding anniversary—we were awakened by the sound of two hummingbirds hovering among the feathery pink blossoms of the silk tree outside our bedroom window.

It was a small sound, more clicks than notes. It had none of the calling beauty of a cardinal's song, for example. And yet we experienced it as a gift, something life offered us for our particular delight.

Any event, when it nourishes our spirits, delights us, brings us energy or vision or direction or courage, is experienced as a gift. It is the genesis of all songs of praise.

Despite objective knowledge, we experience the sense of a gift as highly personal. I know, for example, that Channing did not write his sermon on spiritual freedom hoping that some day in the future someone like me would read it and see more clearly, but when a sentence from the sermon leaps off the page at me, I feel I have been directly addressed. Time has vanished and Channing is speaking his truth into my ear.

In our time it is difficult not to feel guilty about life's gifts, knowing that there are millions for whom a handful of rice would be the most important gift they could receive, knowing that millions are awakened by the sound of guns rather than by two hummingbirds in a silk tree.

A great temptation for the privileged is to ease our guilt by convincing ourselves that we have earned our gifts, by hard work or good deeds or the right creed. Or we go to the other extreme and adopt a kind of spiritual austerity program.

I believe such guilt is fruitless. Our task is to remember three things: gifts that are not received die; gifts that we try to hoard die; gifts that we cannot or do not hand to another die.

The Congregational minister stopped me in the aisle of the supermarket a few months after I had unexpectedly recovered from a serious illness. With a gentle but slightly teasing smile he asked me, "How does a Unitarian deal with a miracle?"

It was a good question, one which I thought about a lot. I started by asking myself more questions.

What is a miracle?

An event that fills us with wonder.

Is a miracle supernatural?

That depends on how one defines supernatural. Traditionally, supernatural has been defined as something beyond the natural, an intervention from outside. But the supernatural also might be defined as that which is most perfectly natural, that which is whole, that which is completely true to its purpose in nature. In this sense, the Eden of the ancient story was supernatural. In this sense, the occasion when a body is allowed to heal itself, and does, is supernatural. Not all bodies will heal themselves. But on those occasions when everything within the wider body is working together—the tremendous skill and caring of the doctors and nurses, the encouragement and love and strength-giving acts of family and friends, the amazing healing powers of the human body itself, and the patient but passionate life-loving spirit within oneself—then this definition of a miracle may apply.

What does a Unitarian Universalist do with a miracle?

She does what all humans do in the presence of wonder. She gives thanks.

My favorite Sabbaths as a child were when my brother and I went with my father to deliver frankfurters and ground beef to the food stand at the amusement park down the street from my father's meat market. The park was one of my favorite places. I loved the merry-go-round, the Tunnel of Love, the Ferris wheel. My mother wouldn't let us ride the roller coaster—there had been too many accidents—but I loved the sound of the wheels on the tracks getting faster and faster and the screams of the people getting louder and louder. Sometimes during the summer, when the wind was just right, I could lie in bed and hear the screams from the roller coaster and the music from the merry-go-round or the dance hall. I thought it was my own special lullaby.

There was something grandly mysterious about being in the park on a Sunday morning when everything was quiet, when we were the only visitors. There was a marvelous sense of waiting, of being in the middle of a deep sleep just before everything awakens. While my father settled the bill with the man at the food stand, my brother and I would run around the park, watching the monkeys in their cages, running from horse to horse on the merry-go-round, or looking at the motionless Ferris wheel, the parked bumper cars, the towering architecture of the roller coaster tracks. It was as if the park was filled with the spirits of people who had been there or were yet to come. But for the moment we were there alone, as if the entire place had been created just for us.

When my father called us, we ran back to the stand. The man who worked there gave us each a candied apple covered with coconut. My father suggested we sit on a bench under one of the maple trees while we ate our apples-on-a-stick.

In the years since I left home I have been in many holy places, from the cathedrals at Canterbury and Chartres to the rim of the Grand Canyon, but I am not sure any were as sacred as that quiet amusement park on summer Sunday mornings in Nebraska. In my heart I am always there, tasting the crispness of apple mingled with the sweetness of sugar syrup and the crunchiness of white coconut, the dappled sunlight touching my face, my father's arm around me, and the entire park waiting there with us, ready to awaken and be filled with life.

I was disappointed to discover recently that students of word origins do not believe that the word "carnival," referring to the festival before Lent, comes from the Italian *carne, vale,* "Oh, flesh, farewell." This is merely folk etymology, they say. The word really comes from two Latin words meaning "the removal of meat"—not nearly as dramatic nor as filled with the sense of solemn sacrifice.

I did not observe Lent until I became a Unitarian Universalist because I had never understood its purpose. In elementary school, when one of my more pious friends asked me what I was giving up for Lent, I responded with the clichés of schoolgirl humor. "Liver, Brussels sprouts, and spelling tests." Much later, I was able to see that giving something up is an attempt to move out of self-concern through a ritual of self-denial.

The theory was that if we sacrificed by fasting or denying ourselves comforts of the body, our spirits would flourish. Yet scripture warns of the danger that self-denial will become self-righteousness. The prophet Isaiah tells us that the true fast is "to loosen the bands of wickedness, to undo the heavy burdens, and to let the oppressed go free. And if thou draw out thy soul to the hungry and satisfy the afflicted soul, then shall thy light rise in obscurity and thy darkness be as the noon day."

Experience teaches us repeatedly that we forget our own egos most quickly when we fully attend to something beyond ourselves. W.H. Auden defines prayer in this way. "To pray is to pay attention to something or someone other than oneself." As he goes on to say, whenever we so concentrate our attention—on a landscape, a poem, a geometrical problem, an idol, or the True God—that we completely forget our own ego and desires, we are praying.

Lent is a time for reflection and prayer, a time not to deny our own needs but to attend to, "to stretch toward," those who are in need of us.

Our fellowship celebrated our traditional flower communion during the Easter service. The huge baskets of daffodils, tulips, lilacs, plum and magnolia branches, and blossoms for which I had no name seemed wondrous analogues of the diverse beauty of the faces of friends and strangers in the congregation. The children, carrying baskets, handed us each a flower with an unusual yet charming seriousness.

I received my daffodil with gratitude, seeing, as always, its radiant yellow as embodied sunlight. Yet driving home though the colorful abundance of an Oregon spring, past house after house with yards filled with daffodils, to our own house and yard filled with daffodils, the wilting flower in my hand began to seem redundant.

I remembered the Christmas our family spent in Finland while my husband was teaching. At Christmas, the Finns have a custom of giving friends pots of blooming spring flowers—hyacinths, tulips, fragrant narcissus. To receive that bright reminder of new life in the midst of the cold and dark of a long Finnish winter was to feel genuinely blessed. When it started to get dark at three in the afternoon, I would brew a cup of tea, sit at the window of our third-floor apartment, look out at the fading light, and smell my blue hyacinths.

Flowers also strengthened my yearning for life during the dark days of a three-month hospital stay with a life-threatening illness. I had always looked on bringing flowers to the sick as a "nice" thing someone like Emily Post had invented. I had not realized how sustaining flowers could be, a loving feast of color for hungry eyes and a gray spirit. I remember awakening after a troubled afternoon sleep and seeing through the haze of pain and myopia the brilliant reds and gold of late summer dahlias left on my bedside table by visitors while I slept. In that first moment, the flowers seemed to be shouting, "Choose life! Choose life!"

At times, like poets and saints, our imaginations are strong enough to keep the presence of flowers alive within us. "Thus I know what a rose is like in winter," Meister Eckhart writes. But when winter is in our souls as well as on the calendar, our imaginations fail us. We welcome the gift of the real rose, the just-picked daffodil, the communion of love that flowers can bring.

The remarkable thing about the Christmas story is the change it represents in human thought. The god who had created the earth in six days, who had brought plagues of frogs and flies, and locusts, and darkness, and the death of the first-born children of Egypt, who had parted the Red Sea and handed down the stone tablets of the law, that god is gone from the old story.

A new story tells of the same god, who needs a humble young woman and the long months of patient waiting and the human process of birth to bring divinity into the world.

That is the part of this quiet story that still speaks to us. Christmas reminds us that the truly divine, the gifts of the spirit, can only enter the world through us. Christmas reminds us that spirit is more than inner feeling; it must be made incarnate in the world as truth spoken, as beauty created, as love and compassion given. Deep joy comes in feeling the quiet, secret movement of the child within us; but the greater joy, and what we are called to do, is to labor to bring forth that child and let it live in the world.

The story may be part history, but to me it is primarily myth. The difference between history and myth is not that one is true and the other is not, but that history is the story of something that happened once thousands of years ago in a faraway country to people we did not know, and myth is the story that happens now, here, in this very place, to every one of us, over and over again. To ask if a myth is true is to ask if the notes on a printed page are music. One can only answer by playing, by singing the music.

A few births are easy. Children arrive almost before we know it. The right words are there on the tip of our tongue. The simple loving act was done spontaneously, almost without thought. But most births are truly acts of labor; some are long and difficult and filled with pain. When the child is born, there are thousands of Herods around us who would slay it through violence or neglect or indifference. Yet our fear of Herod is overcome by the joy of the birth. Rejoice. Rejoice.

For unto us a child is born. And the story of Christmas tells us that we, too, are part of the holiness of creation.

We gather together at the beginning of a new time.

We stand at the edge of a true wilderness. No one has entered it, nor worn a path for us. There are no maps.

We look toward that great openness in awe of the freedom and possibility before us. Yet there is also something in us that causes us to face the unknown territory cautiously and anxiously.

Now, in this place, we take time out of time to look back, to see where we have been and what we have been, to reflect on what we have learned thus far on our journey.

We gather together to remind each other to seek our True North, and to encourage—to place courage in—one another.

When we leave this place, we must each find our true path. We must walk alone.

But now and then we may meet.

When we meet, may we offer each other the bread of our being.

And oh, my brothers, and oh, my sisters, if you hear me plunging wildly, despairingly, through the thicket, call out to me. Calm me.

And if you find me sleeping in the snow, awaken me, lest my heart turn to ice.

And if you hear my music, praising the mornings of the world, then in that other time, in the blackness of my night, sing it back to me. Amen.

We can catch glimpses of who we are by looking at our historical past, as a demonination and as a fellowship. To know who we are, we must know where we came from and which ideas moved us. The nature of Unitarian Universalism is constantly changing and we have no creed; yet certain ideas have existed throughout our history.

We have always believed that the source of religious authority does not reside in the Pope, or the minister, or in a book, but within the center of our own personalities, within our deepest selves. That idea has often been corrupted to suggest that all expressions of belief are equally valid.

We have always believed in freedom of thought and the expression of thought. That idea has been corrupted so that it often seems to be saying, "Leave me alone," rather than "Tell me what you see." We have always been advocates of religious tolerance, but that belief has changed from saying, "I won't burn you at the stake," to saying, "I won't let you know I disagree with you."

In the great religious division between those who would exclude in order to purify and those who would embrace in order to redeem, we have always been with the embracers. We have no creedal requirements for membership, which is how it should be, but that does not mean we should not be passionate about our search for truth, nor that membership has no meaning.

My friend, Maggie, was working in her kitchen one afternoon when she overheard her young son talking with a classmate who had come to play after school. In the midst of milk and cookies, the visitor, who came from a Catholic family, began to talk about communion.

"What's communion?" David, her son, asked, as any Unitarian Universalist child would.

"Oh," his friend responded, "it's where you go to a special place in the church and they give you bread and wine."

David's face lit up with delight and understanding. "Oh, yes," he said. "We have that too, only we call it potluck."

I laughed when Maggie told me that story, but I've thought about it often and see a truth in it. I suspect the final supper that Jesus had with his friends resembled a potluck more than the rite of the Eucharist. At times I have experienced a UU potluck that partook of communion, a time when the occasion was infused with love. Not all potlucks are communions, of course. Few are. But then not all communions are communions.

Still, there is a spiritual meeting and nourishment that calls for the name "communion," and it bothers me that we have so readily given up the concept as well as the word. Instead of trying to reclaim religious words, to rediscover their underlying meaning, we merely throw them out.

I believe there is such a thing as communion, though it is not necessarily a religious rite at the altar of a church. There are times that are truly holy—sacred—Sabbaths, but the setting aside of one day a week and naming it the Sabbath is merely a symbolic reminder of the true Sabbaths of our lives. My confirmation did not take place when I was fourteen, after a class at the Presbyterian church. Rather, when I was fifty-nine years old, desperately ill, facing death and excruciating pain, yet embraced by love and intelligence, everything in which I had professed to trust was verified and strengthened by the experience. I never hesitate to call that my confirmation.

God is writing a poem.
I am one of the words.
He utters me.

(Do I mean what He means me to mean?)

THE POET GOD

When God's voice stops,
When the poem is finished,
The poem will be.
I will be.

(Do you think poems die? They are completed.
Do you think we die? We complete the poem.)

Without me, the poem would not be whole.
Without the poem, my word is hollow sound.
Without God, nothing.

(The world goes mad with noise.
We cannot hear ourselves.
God, sing in our ears again.)

When I was giving birth to Shana, when my body was seized by a force I could not control but only accept, I had the notion that Life was using me, that I was merely the channel for a mighty river rushing through me to an unknown sea. I could not direct it, slow it, hasten it—all I could do, need do, was say "yes."

Later, when life cried, "Help me," when my will seemed joined with my body again, when my muscles, energy, strength, courage, self were all working together toward that moment of Shana's first liberation, when Dr. George said, "Bear down now, Charlotte," and Nick, looking strange in his white smock, said, "I love you, Charlotte," that was when I knew the beginning of joy. The truth that I heard in that first rebellious cry was this: Life needs me for its becoming.

Father, sometimes I know myself as a cemetery filled with dead ideas, dead images, dead love. Father, sometimes I want to weep for all the moments life cried, "Help me," and I would not hear. Then it is as if a voice says, "Hush. Stop crying, child. Listen to the song." Is that what you sang to me, father, long ago in the moonlight?

(This "song" is from a short story, "My Father's Lullabies," in which the narrator, Charlotte, composes a series of lullabies to comfort her aging father as he had comforted her when she was a child.)

I

No love among the mourners. Let us cry.
Death came like a tear, something for the eyes
To lose, furrowing the face, bitter in the mouth,
Soft smallness without piety or fear.
And when we asked the headlines, they could only
    say:
At Buchenwald death crouched upon the floor;
Hiroshima found death could die no more.
They would be right and wrong. When
Is a useless question. Let us all ignore
Confusion and the clock. Let us call
Death death, not ask when death, or where.
Each finds the knowledge, lying in his bed.
Each raises shade to resurrect the sky
But finds no anger there, no penitence, no dread,
No love among the mourners. Let us cry.

II

Giotto knew. A scheme of light and shadow and
The understanding of a gentle hand.

Giotto knew. When Mary placed her arm across his
    breast,
The two embraced the pity of the rest.

Giotto knew abstractions have no breath
And brought to life by representing death.

No love among the mourners and a few
Must ask what lonely thing is dying. Giotto knew.

III

Like the chapel, his was no beautiful
Exterior. Bad jokes, six ugly children,
Even Dante laughed. His teacher found
Him drawing pictures in the dusty ground.
Freed from the cloister, what would the love
Be, the devout drama of the cross?
Giotto knew what pity was about.
Only his art would bring the inside out.

IV

No motion to accept or deny;
No love among the mourners. Let us cry.

*(Written after a "sacred encounter" with a book on
the Giotto frescoes, a book which also described the
role Giotto played in bringing humanness into his
depiction of the divine.)*

It is as important for members of a fellowship to get away together as it is for a family or a couple. We too often get caught in routine questions—how to balance the budget, when to repair the gutters, what to do with the fifty-nine extra zucchini—that we lose sight of our purposes and each other. Then a great need arises to make space in time, to take a space in space, not merely to have fun together, but to see each other anew, or to meet each other for the first time.

I come home from such events as the Beverly Beach Campout with a collage of images rather than a chronology of events. I look into the kaleidoscope of memory and see Nini and Heather T. perched high on their father's shoulders; Brendan in the firelight, toasting miniature marshmallows for the benefit of the bugs; and a myriad of kites in the Saturday afternoon sky (including my prized thirty-six-foot dragon, given to me by the Burnett children to thank me for "doing that thing where you sprinkled the water").

I can hear the rustle of kites in the strong wind. I can hear Vivian's laughter. I can hear Tane and John reciting their boy's-camp-version of "The Three Bears." I can hear the voices of Carl and Cosmo, Kermit and Allen around the campfire late at night. I can hear Henry and Heather playing "Go Tell Aunt Rhody" on their recorders.

I see Janet in her pointed red hat and Vivian in her red nightgown and Jory, the young girl in the blue velvet top and new jeans. I see Art staggering from his tent Sunday morning looking, some might say, like the wrath of God, though it strikes me more as the look of God's beleaguered servant. I see us standing in the campground in the morning sun, looking up through Bob's binoculars at the black bird preening itself at the top of a tall fir while, in a mirroring motion below, the men are combing their hair and their beards. I see Judy and Heather W., with knives and cutting boards, revealing the inner secrets of potatoes and squash.

I see the faces of Janet, Carl, and Vivian as we stand at the water's edge in the waning light of Saturday. The gray is still luminous enough to make us understand clearly that it is not that the light is disappearing but we are turning away from it. I see the two planets hanging on the horizon. I see the driftwood totem upright in the sand silhouetted in the twilight. I hear the fall of the wood as a careless beach-walker shoves it over. I hear in Carl's voice the gift of selfless anger. I see him run to right the wood again, like Jacob raising the stone at Bethel. I see the faces of my friends. I see them.

The visions that we have for our religious community are sometimes muddied by trivia, by too much talk of organizational flow charts and too little talk of people, ideas, and purposes—by too little sharing of our depths and our dreams. We need to get away now and then—to see each other anew—to ask anew who we are, what we are called to do, and how we may best love one another.

"Today if ye will hear his voice, harden not your heart."
—Psalms 95:7-8

As a child I always thought the "hardened heart" of the Bible meant the heart was frozen. To me it always suggested sternness, cruelty, anger. Experience has taught me that the slow coming of the ice is more subtle, that there are times one doesn't recognize it has happened until the moment of the thaw. Experience has taught me that this freezing often does not reflect hostility or hatred, but a quieter kind of defense—a defense against too much life, against the possibility of pain, against self-knowledge.

Still, even in the quiet, there are signs—inertia or frantic activity, boredom, self-pity, the failure to respond authentically to the suffering of another, even though one may go through the motions of kindness. But when the thaw comes, it brings with it the joy and pain of life restored. Life flows in us and through us. We are no longer exiled from ourselves.

And what can thaw us, open us into the fullness of our being? Like spring in Nebraska, the thaw can come as the strong warm power of the sun rising out of the darkness, or as the sudden breaking through the icy crust by the force of truth.

For me, at various times, it has been the wildness of Big Bend Park, or the ever-changing light of the skies of New Mexico, or the silver-gray Oregon Coast— the small loving act of a seeing friend, a sentence on a page shouting up at me, the solace of solitude or of the harmonies of music, a child's question, an artist's vision, a teacher's demand—those moments of real meaning, those moments when grief is accepted, those moments which cannot be defined except by the religious word "grace," when ordinary acts are lifted up to take on new meaning, and all of life becomes sacramental.

I wasn't flattered when one of my daughters confided that she had thought of me as "The Big There-There" when she was three years old. If I remember correctly, I was in the middle of a phase where I was hoping to reassure myself that I still had a fertile mind as well as a welcoming bosom.

Now, years later, I can admit that the role of Big There-There is a necessary part of parenthood not to be disparaged. At times even the most mature of us want someone to dry our eyes, encircle us with welcoming arms, and offer us a cup of hot cocoa. I shall be forever grateful to my friend Ruth, who interrupted her political campaign to ride to the hospital, make her way past the folks in intensive care with convincing stories that I was her little sister, and reach bravely through the thicket of I.V.s, heart monitors, and breathing tubes to embrace me.

Still, the origin of the word "comfort" means "to make strong." As comforters, we often believe we have to take away the pain, only to discover that we are only able to help those in pain find the sources of their own strength. At times it is our mere presence. "I am here. I see your suffering. I care for you." At times it is a helping hand. "I'll vacuum. I'll wash up these dishes. I'll drive you." At times, it is a few words that put things in perspective.

We're never quite sure what will truly comfort another, or what special act will comfort us. We go looking for a "Big There-There" and find instead that the excitement of a new idea lifts us from despair. I expected little solace from my frail ninety-year-old father when he called me in the hospital to see how I was, but when he called me "Punky" for the first time in fifty-four years, I felt the fidelity of that relationship. My narrow room was filled with memory and hope.

Perhaps those of us who would be comforters could learn from the medieval scholastic who wrote so long ago, "Work, therefore, in what you do, from love and not from fear."

If we can put aside our fear that we might say or do something to add inadvertently to the suffering of those we would comfort, if we can put aside our fear of our own loss or the pain of our own pity, then love might find its way of bringing strength to the weak and light to those in the shadows.

When solving a double acrostic, I love that moment, usually about the ninth clue, when suddenly everything falls into place and I know the puzzle will be solved.

Having struggled with the theological puzzle of "evil" for most of my life, I had that same kind of "aha" experience when, partway through a book on process theology by John Cobb and David Ray Griffin, I encountered the idea that two kinds of experiences are equally evil—triviality and discord.

For centuries, considerations of the problems of evil have focused primarily on physical and mental suffering, ignoring the possibility that overcoming unnecessary triviality may be equally important.

This idea seemed to explain why I gave two grades on each theme when I taught freshman composition classes at the university. It was the only way to deal with the young woman who wrote meaningless essays with perfect punctuation and grammar and the young man sitting next to her whose images stunned me into awareness and whose ideas, though expressed in a muddy maze of misspelled words, had an exciting freshness.

It explained why I had met people who seemed largely free of greed, gluttony, sloth, and the other deadly sins, but whose lives seemed pretty empty. It explained why we fear Big Brother, even if Big Brother might bring an end to discord. It explained why I mourn the fact that the shelves of the most beautiful room in our new public library are lined with paperback romances and that many churches have replaced Gregorian chants, Bach, Mozart, and Charles Ives with songs that sound like greeting card verse set to telephone commercial tunes.

We are living in an age of uncommon discord. No wonder we are afraid, and many of us try to escape our fear through trivial pursuits of all kinds: trivial television rather than the restorative gift of genuine play; trivial sex rather than the complex beauty of relationships that are whole; trivial sloganeering instead of the real thought and clarifying exchange of honest political dialogue; trivial puzzles rather than the real puzzles of a real existence.

According to Cobb and Griffin, "The divine reality, who not only enjoys all enjoyments but suffers all sufferings, is an Adventurer." May we, too, be adventurers.

We bring you this morning the ancient story of the Nativity.

We ask you to listen to this story as if for the first time—before symbol was petrified into dogma—before myth was mistaken for history.

Paul Tillich wrote: "The first step toward the non-religion of the Western world was made by religion itself. When it defended its great symbols not as symbols but as literal stories, it had already lost the battle."

Imagine, that this ancient story is radically new.

Imagine, that after years of hearing story after story of men and women bowing abjectly before the might of kings and emperors, tsars, dictators, chieftains, and tyrants, you hear a story in which three kings kneel before a tiny child—in praise of possibility.

Imagine, that after hearing story after story of long wars and bloody battles and heroes slaying their enemies, bombings and burnings and persecutions and pogroms, you one day hear the quiet story of a birth, the story of the humble carpenter and his gentle wife, shepherds in the starlit fields, animals in a stable, the story of the deep human longing for peace.

Imagine that you are hearing for the first time a story that questions the assumption that power resides in armies and armadas, witches and wizards, and magic swords and sacks of gold. Imagine that you hear a story that affirms the strong, transforming power of love.

Imagine the day when everyone who hears the story and says "I believe" will be talking about the meaning, not the plot.

We bring to you now that ancient story, that ever-new story. Listen to the story.

We light this flame in remembrance of our ancestors who kindled bonfires on the barren hills of winter to beg the sun to stay alive, to give it strength for its return.

We light this flame in remembrance of those ancient people who each New Year's Day carried new fire into their homes to cleanse them and purify them and make them new.

We light this flame in gratitude to all those people who from the depth of history have carried the light of life into this moment, who have preserved and handed on life's radiant beauty.

We light this flame in affirmation of the light that dwells within each of us, the light that is part of the one light.

We are not asked to look at the Light; we are asked to look at, and love, and praise, and heal the world this Light illumines.

Recently I reread the story of the first Sabbath, trying to approach it with the freshness of a seven-year-old mind, as I might have first read about Dr. Doolittle or the Wizard of Oz. In my seven-year-old persona, my first question was this: "What did God do on the Sabbath?" For those of us growing up in traditional religions, the talk was about what we shouldn't do. We shouldn't play cards. We shouldn't go to movies. We were told what we should stay away from, not what we should move toward.

Both the story and my own experience suggested that on that first Sabbath, along with resting, God was undoubtedly experiencing post-creation euphoria. Anyone who has written a story—or painted a picture, baked an elegant chocolate torte, built a house, made a quilt, or had a baby—can identify with God the creator. What has always delighted me is that after the second day and the third day and the fourth day, God looked at what he had done and saw that it was good, but after the sixth day he looked at all that he had done and saw that it was very good. It was only later that, like all other creators, he began to notice the flaws—the serpent beguiling Eve, Cain killing Abel. Indeed, by the sixth chapter of Genesis, God was repenting that he had ever started the whole thing. (Every creator can recognize this moment.)

But God spent the first Sabbath seeing the creation in all its harmony, blessing it and loving it. He needed to recognize and celebrate its value, which is the original meaning of worship.

I often forget that the first act of worship on the earth was God's worship of the creation, not the other way around.

One of the things I learned during a long, life-threatening illness was how much the will to live is related to how much pain we are willing—or able—to accept. Saying "yes" to life is inevitably saying "yes" to pain. The joy of friendship or marriage always contains the seed of the inevitability of final separation. The joy of creation always contains the risk of pain.

Any creative person—writer, minister, parent, painter— must risk different kinds of pain.

There is the risk of failure—your work does not live up to your vision.

There is the risk of obstruction. You finish your work, and it is the work you intended it to be, but something stands between you and those you would give it to. The censor. The lack of resources to bring it to the others. The whims of the marketplace. And at the other end, the indifference of those you hoped would receive it. Closed minds, closed eyes, closed hearts.

There is the risk of rejection—that force-filled word from the Latin *iacere,* "to throw back."

Finally, there is the risk of annihilation, with that huge "nothing" in the middle. Writers have an edge here. Since there are multiple copies of their work, book burners don't usually get them all. Still, only seven of Sophocles' plays survive—though he wrote well over a hundred. The manuscript can be lost. The cathedral can be bombed. The community can decay. The child can die.

It is part of the wisdom of words that "aesthetic" and "anesthetic" are opposites. Those very words ask the question: How much pain are we willing to risk to feel keenly the beauty that life offers?

When our fellowship decided we wanted a minister, I'm not sure we agreed, or even knew, what we meant by that. Perhaps most of us wanted a surrogate rather than a minister—someone who would stand in the pulpit and say those things each of us would say if we were willing to struggle with the concepts and images that would articulate our individual truths; someone who would walk into society and fight the battles we would fight if we had the courage to risk our jobs and reputations and physical well-being; someone who would visit the sick and despairing for us and bring them the comfort we would bring if we had the love to endure the suffering and the drudgery that such comforting sometimes involves. I suspect most of us regarded religion, to the extent we regarded it at all, as a spectator sport.

In some sense the idea of the surrogate stayed with us when we were between ministers—sometimes defined as the board or the program committee, occasionally as the president, but most often as a vague, mysterious "they." We all know well that the surrogate concept causes innumerable problems in the era of ministerial leadership, as the congregation slowly discovers that ministers are their own persons who wish to show us their own visions of truth and walk in the world in their own ways. But the continuation of this concept in an era of a "do it ourselves" fellowship damns that fellowship to sterility.

"Surrogatism" is manifested when a minister leaves and a number of the most devoted followers leave as well. I admit that while I empathize with the impulse, I cannot understand the act. It reminds me of an orchestra where all the strings stop playing at the death of the concertmaster and then leave in despair because their beloved orchestra has started to sound like a band. For those to whom the minister was more than a Sunday-morning diversion, the absence of the one who provoked or enticed or inspired them into their own search for meaning surely makes their own presence in the community essential—to articulate that meaning, to enter into dialogue, and thus to provoke, entice, or inspire others.

Surrogatism occurs in every committee meeting where someone sits in silence for two hours and spends two hours after the meeting complaining about what "they" have decided, in every coffee hour where someone chats with an old friend the entire time, ignoring the richness of strangers, and then nods vigorously at the old cliche that "UUs are cold." It occurs on all those occasions when someone who has been a member for two years or five years or longer than I have says, "Why don't you people ever . . ." rather than, "We ought to . . ." It happens when those who hate drabness do not bring color, and those who hate darkness do not bring light.

It is scary to start the dance. One often finds oneself alone in the middle of the floor. It is scary to speak one's truth. One is usually misunderstood, often not listened to, occasionally laughed at. But until each of us is willing to risk that for the sake of the others, I do not believe we shall have genuine meeting. Dialogue is something one enters into; it is not something that can be provided for us. The fellowship will only come to life with the death of our dependence on the surrogate.

I have always lacked enthusiasm for Mother's Day when I am the mother involved.

Birthdays are different. Birthdays are about who I am inside, and what my history walking this earth has been—what someone has called "the majesty of particular existence." I'm pleased when people tell me they're glad they have shared some of that life with me and would like to share more. But I tend to think of a Mother's Day celebration as a generic birthday party.

I suppose my lukewarm feeling toward the day began when my children were very young and each year served me lukewarm eggs for a "surprise" breakfast in bed. Sitting in solitary splendor with my glass of skim milk rather than my usual steaming coffee, I would much rather have been downstairs with the rest of the family, giggling around the dining room table.

But the older I get, the stronger understanding grows of how many people have helped to create and to nourish my children's bodies and spirits. I feel silly being singled out for praise when I remember the gifted teachers who inspired them, the adult friends who comforted them, their comrades throughout the years who have loved them and challenged them and kept them singing.

If we're going to observe the day, let's recognize that as parents we did not raise our children by ourselves. Let us remember, as children, how many people it took to bring our being into existence.

Let us praise those who have created us and bequeathed to us the gifts of life. Let us praise our mother and our father for our genetic legacy and for the care they have given us.

But let us also praise those who have preserved and passed on our great cultural heritage. Let us praise those who have nourished us physically, but also those who have stimulated our minds and fed our spirits; those who have created a home for us, but those also who labor so long to make the world more homelike. As we praise these people, let us vow to hand down this legacy, not merely to our own children, but to all the children of the earth.

During the hot Nebraska summers of my childhood, I spent hours, high in my treehouse, devouring the books I found in the small collection my parents had acquired from the estates of various relatives.

One of my favorites was *A Wonder Book,* Nathaniel Hawthorne's retelling of classical myths. My favorite of those stories was "The Miraculous Pitcher," the story of Baucis and Philemon. This elderly, poor, but generous-hearted couple invite two gods, disguised as beggars, to come into their cottage to rest and eat. The gods keep asking that their bowls be replenished, and the old couple become sad and embarrassed because they know the pitcher is empty. But the gods show them otherwise. No matter how often they pour from the pitcher, it is always full.

I suppose that as a child, what I liked was the thought of possessing such a pitcher. Much later I realized that in some sense I did. The story of the miraculous pitcher seems to be telling us that in the realm of the spirit there is no such thing as a non-renewable resource.

That is an important concept. Most of us have it backward. For centuries we have had it backward. We have believed that material resources are infinite but the resources of the spirit need to be hoarded with care. We act as if the supply of oil can go on forever but that there are limits to the amount of love we can give away. How often I have found myself closing off from people in need because I was afraid of being spiritually drained, only to find myself in the driest of deserts.

We have arrived at a time in our history when we are beginning to realize that this planet is our only home; we can no longer make a mess of the place where we are and then move on. A species can come to an end. Resources can be used up. All growth is not a sign of health.

But I suspect we doubt more than ever the truth in the story of the miraculous pitcher—or the loaves and the fishes. We find it hard to believe that we will find the spiritual nourishment to meet the needs of this chaotic age.

The wisdom of the centuries and our own experience tell us otherwise. If we do not let our fears have dominion, we may discover that in the midst of pain we find inner strength, in the midst of bewilderment we find inner clarity, in the midst of nourishing another we find ourselves nourished.

Visiting my son and his family one November, I awakened the first morning to the wonderful sounds of a house coming to life, to that once-familiar chaos of getting off to school, the sounds of small feet in the hallway, flushings and brushings, showerings and scourings, and the occasional loud whisper, "Shhh! Grandma's still asleep."

When I hear the last of the feet going down the stairs to breakfast, I venture into the bathroom, push aside the large collection of boats, pails, frogs, ducks, and fish in the bottom of the tub, and take my shower. Putting on my warmest sweater and my old wool slacks, I go down to greet them, to have my communal bowl of Cheerios, and to help in the final search for the missing jacket, the hidden shoe, the perfect thing for Show and Tell before they hurry out to the road to catch the schoolbus. Then I pour myself a cup of coffee and sit down with the mildly exhausted Mom and Dad to enjoy the sudden splendid silence of the morning.

I am swept by a wave of nostalgia that surprises me. I have become so fond of the solitude of early morning that it seems strange to find that part of me misses the chaos. I realize that I probably no longer have the agile energy that would allow me to wander safely through that chaos for very long. Still, in the midst of the final movement of life's symphony, I miss the scherzo.

I suppose that is why I sometimes go to both services on Christmas Eve—the one in which the toddlers wander in the aisles, babies sometimes cry, and the beginning violinists join the motley orchestra that accompanies the carols; the one in quiet candlelight, where one can hear every note of the skilled musicians, every word of the poet's wisdom, where one can even sit in moments of rich silence and reflect on the meaning of the season.

Scientists studying the growth and uniqueness of snow-flakes have found two things: the laws of pattern formation are universal and the final flake records the history of all the changing weather conditions it has experienced. Perhaps this represents a religious truth as well as a scientific one. In solitude we intuit the intended pattern of human growth (what once was called "the voice of God"). In experiencing the turbulent weather of life and responding to it, we become our own unique selves.

On our last Sunday in Greece a few summers ago, we were awakened by church bells in the mountain village where we were staying. After breakfast on the sunny courtyard of the guesthouse, we drove down to Volos to see the museum.

In one room we stood beside the tomb of a six-year-old girl who had lived—and died—in the fourth century B.C.E. We looked at the things that had been placed in the stone coffin with her—a doll, a pair of sandals blackened by decay, a purple tunic, a small vessel to hold the tears of the mourners. Our guide told us that there was also evidence of food that had been left there—chestnuts, hazelnuts, apples, and pomegranates.

It seemed strange to feel a pang of sorrow for a death that had taken place twenty-four centuries ago, one death of an unknown child among anguished billions of deaths. But looking again at the small vial that had once held tears, it was clear that the pain was not for the child, but for those she had left behind, those who had placed the doll and the apple beside her in that final act of grief-struck love.

Something within us wanted to call out across vast fields of time and space, "We know. We know. All humans come to know. There is no vessel large enough to hold the tears of love."

As much as we Unitarian Universalists stress freedom of religion and praise diversity of thought, I suspect it takes most of us a long time to feel comfortable discovering our differences and even longer before we can celebrate them with enthusiasm.

Our initial excitement about our congregations often comes from the feeling that we have at last found people who think like us. When we discover that that might not be entirely the case, we often focus on what we have in common and try to avoid exploring differences that we fear will divide us.

I remember my own excitement when I discovered that "diverse" means "turned in different ways." The root meaning of the word expresses so clearly the strength we can find in diversity, the way the vision of another can enhance our own. On the other hand, to "divide" means "to force apart." Because we fear that expressing our diversity will lead to division, we often retreat into silence (or express our own views so forcefully that others retreat into silence) rather than engaging in the genuine dialogue that will enrich us all.

On occasions when I have been able to explore with another person just where we differ, when we have both had the trust—and the time—to tell each other what we have seen and how we have come to understand it, I have found the experience to be energizing and clarifying. My thought is clarified, but the boundaries of my self are also clarified. I am more sure what is the "me" and what is the "not me." And I have found myself in some way bound to the person who is seeking with me. The person who had seemed to be my opponent has suddenly become my partner.

Over the years I have come to believe that the meeting of minds, in loving argument as well as in common purpose, is both creative and holy.

Camping our way through Europe when our children were small, my husband and I were persuaded by the chorus of their eager voices to take them to the maze at Hampton Court, just outside of London. We drove there one summer afternoon and started exploring, each of us separately walking along the hedge-lined paths.

Often I could hear a recognizable voice on the other side of the hedge or would meet a familiar face coming back from a blind alley, as we searched the paths with a group of strangers—some laughing, some anxious, some impatient—all of us together in this puzzle. Suddenly the meaning of what we were doing seemed to expand beyond the paths we were walking, into our lives.

When I finally reached the center of the maze and found people sitting on benches in the sun, quietly talking, laughing, sharing apples out of a backpack, it was with a mixture of surprise and recognition—surprise because I had had it in my head that a maze was something to get through rather than to find the center of—recognition, partly because I had once seen a diagram of Hampton Court, but primarily because the experience seemed "true" in some way.

I remembered how that morning I had pored over the guidebook worrying about whether we would have time to do all the sights in the few days remaining. I remembered sorrowfully leaving my favorite Botticelli painting because of the strange sense of obligation to see as many rooms of the museum as I could.

Many times in the years since that lovely August day that memory has come back to me. When I find myself hurrying through an experience, trying to solve or finish it rather than immersing myself in it and giving full attention to the moment, I often remember the maze. Then I remind myself, "It is the center you are looking for, that timeless moment in the noonday sun."

The most important question anyone ever asked me (besides "Will you marry me?") was asked by our first minister the day after I had met with two unhappy and somewhat hostile members of the congregation who didn't like some of the decisions of the program committee I was chairing.

"Well, Barbara, what did you learn from that?"

The question startled me. In his place I would have asked, "How was it?" or "How did it go?," meaning, "Was it terribly unpleasant?" or "Did it turn out the way you hoped it would?" or even (I blush to admit) "Did you win?"

His question helped me recognize that there are more profitable ways of looking at my experience than evaluating it in terms of pleasure or pain, or how well it conformed to the scenario I had written in my head.

I began, in the following months and years, to ask myself more frequently, "How did this experience change me and the world around me? What did this experience tell me about the nature of reality?"

I began to find that my life suffered unless I maintained a balance of action and contemplation. I found it difficult to possess my experience unless I took time to reflect upon it. I have become addicted to keeping a journal. Although my journal often contains a factual account of an experience, or expresses the myriad of feelings that accompany that experience, more often I use the journal to search for the meaning within the experience, to understand what the experience says to the rest of my life.

Little by little, I am learning that it is not enough merely to taste life to see if it is sweet or bitter. One must discover the nourishing kernel of truth within one's experience and make it part of one's self.

Barbara Rohde grew up in Nebraska, graduated from Carleton College, and lived in Illinois, Florida, Ohio, and North Dakota, before moving to Oregon and discovering the Unitarian Universalist Fellowship of Corvallis. She has been an active member of the Corvallis congregation since 1967. Her poetry, short stories, personal essays, and book reviews have appeared in a variety of national publications. She is also the author of a previously published collection of essays, *Seeking For Our True North*. She is married to Kermit, a social psychologist, and they have four children and three grandchildren.

ABOUT THE AUTHOR

Unitarians and Universalists have been publishing annual editions of prayer collections and meditation manuals for 150 years. In 1841 the Unitarians broke with their tradition of addressing only theological topics and published *Short Prayers for the Morning and Evening of Every Day in the Week, with Occasional Prayers and Thanksgivings*. Over the years, the Unitarians published many volumes of prayers, including Theodore Parker's selections. In 1938 *Gaining a Radiant Faith* by Henry H. Saunderson launched the current tradition of an annual Lenten manual.

Several Universalist collections appeared in the early nineteenth century. A comprehensive *Book of Prayers* was published in 1839, featuring both public and private devotions. During the late 1860s, the Universalist Publishing House was founded to publish denominational materials. Like the Unitarians, the Universalists published Lenten manuals, and in the 1950s they complemented this series with Advent manuals.

Since 1961, the year the Unitarians and the Universalists merged, the Lenten manual has evolved into a meditation manual, reflecting the theological diversity of the two denominations. Today the Unitarian Universalist Association meditation manuals include two styles of collections: poems or short prose pieces written by one author—usually a Unitarian Universalist minister—and anthologies of works by many authors.

The following list includes all meditation manuals since the merger, plus most titles prior to 1961.

Unitarian Universalist

1993   *Life Tides* Elizabeth Tarbox[‡]

       The Gospel of Universalism
          Tom Owen-Towle[‡]

1992   *Noisy Stones* Robert R. Walsh[‡]

1991 *Been in the Storm So Long* Mark Morrison-
Reed and Jacqui James, Editors[‡]

1990 *Into the Wilderness* Sara Moores Campbell[‡]

1989 *A Small Heaven* Jane Ranney Rzepka[‡]

1988 *The Numbering of Our Days*
Anthony Friess Perrino[‡]

1987 *Exaltation* David B. Parke, Editor[‡]

1986 *Quest* Kathy Fuson Hurt[‡]

1985 *The Gift of the Ordinary*
Charles S. Stephen, Jr., Editor

1984 *To Meet the Asking Years*
Gordon B. McKeeman, Editor

1983 *Tree and Jubilee* Greta W. Crosby

1981 *Outstretched Wings of the Spirit*
Donald S. Harrington

1980 *Longing of the Heart* Paul N. Carnes

1979 *Portraits from the Cross* David Rankin

1978 *Songs of Simple Thanksgiving*
Kenneth L. Patton

1977 *The Promise of Spring* Clinton Lee Scott

1976 *The Strangeness of This Business*
Clarke D. Wells

1975 *In Unbroken Line* Chris Raible, Editor

1974 *Stopping Places* Mary Lou Thompson

1973 *The Tides of Spring* Charles W. Grady

1972 *73 Voices* Chris Raible and
Ed Darling, Editors

1971 *Bhakti, Santi, Love, Peace* Jacob Trapp

1970 *Beginning Now* J. Donald Johnston

[‡] These meditation manuals are available from the
Unitarian Universalist Association. For a free catalog,
write to the UUA Bookstore, 25 Beacon St., Boston,
MA 02108-2800.

1969 *Answers in the Wind* Charles W. McGehee

1968 *The Trying Out* Richard Kellaway

1967 *Moments of Springtime* Rudolf Nemser

1966 *Across the Abyss* Walter D. Kring

1965 *The Sound of Silence* Raymond Baughan

1964 *Impassioned Clay* Ralph Helverson

1963 *Seasons of the Soul* Robert T. Weston

1962 *The Uncarven Image* Phillip Hewett

1961 *Parts and Proportions* Arthur Graham

Council of Liberal Churches (Universalist-Unitarian)

1960 *Imprints of the Divine* Raymond Hopkins

1959 *Indictments and Invitations* Robert B. Cope

1958 *Strange Beauty* Vincent Silliman

1957 *Greatly to Be* Francis Anderson, Jr.

1956 *My Heart Leaps Up* Frank O. Holmes

Unitarian

1955 *The Task Is Peace* Harry Scholefield

1954 *Taking Down the Defenses* Arthur Foote

1953 *My Ample Creed* Palfrey Perkins

1952 *This Man Jesus* Harry C. Meserve

1951 *The Tangent of Eternity* John Wallace Laws

1950 *Deep Sources and Great Becoming*
       Edwin C. Palmer

1949 *To Take Life Strivingly* Robert Killan

1948 *Come Up Higher* Hurley Begun

1947 *Untitled* Richard Steiner

1946 *The Pattern on the Mountain* (reissue)
       E. Burdette Backus

1945 *The Expendable Life* Charles G. Girelius

1944   *The Disciplines of Freedom*
        Leslie T. Pennington

1943   *Faith Forbids Fear* Frederick May Eliot

1942   *Forward into the Light* Frederick W. Griffin

1941   *Victorious Living* W. W. W. Argow

1940   *Address to the Living* Herbert Hitchen

1939   *The Pattern on the Mountain*
        E. Burdette Backus

1938   *Gaining a Radiant Faith*
        Henry H. Saunderson

Universalist

1955   *Heritages* Harmon M. Gehr

1954   *Words of Life* Albert F. Ziegler

1953   *Wisdom About Life* Tracy M. Pullman

1952   *Spiritual Embers* John E. Wood

1951   *The Breaking of Bread*
        Raymond John Baughan

1950   *Add to Your Faith* Roger F. Etz

1949   *To Take Life Strivingly* Robert Killam

1948   *Of One Flame* Robert Cummins

1947   *Using Our Spiritual Resources* Roger F. Etz

1946   *A New Day Dawns*
        Walter Henry Macpherson

1945   *Beauty for Ashes* Robert and Elsie Barber

1944   *The Price of Freedom* Edson R. Miles

1943   *The Ladder of Excellence* Frank D. Adams

1942   *The Whole Armor of God* Donald B.F. Hoyt

1941   *Earth's Common Things* Max A. Kapp

1940   *The Interpreter* Frederic W. Perkins

1939   *The Great Avowal* Horace Westwood

1938   *Add to Your Faith* Roger F. Etz